THE
LITTLE
BOOK OF
STRESS

THE LITTLE BOOK OF
STRESS

Rohan Candappa

Andrews McMeel
Publishing

Kansas City

First publication by Ebury Press in Great Britain 1998

The Little Book of Stress copyright © 2000 by Rohan Candappa.
All rights reserved. Printed in the United States of America.
No part of this book may be used or reproduced in any
manner whatsoever without written permission except
in the case of reprints in the context of reviews.
For information, write Andrews McMeel Publishing,
an Andrews McMeel Universal company,
4520 Main Street, Kansas City, Missouri 64111.

01 02 03 04 BIN 10 9 8 7 6

ISBN: 0-7407-0474-5

Library of Congress Catalog Card Number: 99-67129

Stress. Is it really all bad? Or is it just misunderstood? Perhaps its only crime is to have fallen foul of a conspiracy of namby-pamby, New Age do-gooders. Well, enough is enough. It's time to put the record straight.

Time to proclaim the most radical philosophical truth. Time to admit that stress is good. Because without stress we would all be very, very, very nice. And stomach-churningly contented. And, in all honesty, who wants to live in a world like that?

The simple teachings I have collected in this little book show you how to increase the level of stress both within you and those around you. It is by no means a definitive guide. But it is a start. I hope you find it useful.

THE REMOTE CONTROL
STRATAGEM

Find out when your friends'
favorite TV program is on.
Then call them seven minutes
after it starts.

HUSBAND YOUR RESOURCES

When you ask a woman any question, suggest she checks with her husband before answering.

This is even more productive if you are a woman yourself.

EVEN IN YOUR SLEEP YOU CAN GENERATE STRESS

Learn to snore.

IT'S QUICKER BY TUBE

Squeeze the toothpaste tube from
the middle.

Never replace the cap.

TAKE FIZZICAL EXERCISE

Whenever you have the opportunity,
shake up cans and bottles of fizzy drinks.
Then leave them for someone else to open.

THE WAITING GAME

Always be late.

FRIENDS

Choose friends you don't like.

FAN THE FLAMES

Always join in other people's arguments.
Try to get others to join in, too.

PRACTICE BUTTON
PUSHING

If you have free time during the rush hour,
find a pedestrian crossing and repeatedly
push the button to stop the traffic.
Never actually cross the road.

DON'T CHANGE

Never have the right change for anything.

THE MILK OF
HUMAN UNKINDNESS

Put empty milk cartons back in the fridge.

FROM GREEN TO RED

When you're the first car in line at
a traffic light, get out and read a map.
Try to miss the green light at least twice.

LATE AGAIN

If you're enjoying a physical relationship
with a new man, give it a few weeks and
then tell him you've missed your period.

This information is best left on
an answering machine.

Be foreign

Be German. Or whatever . . .

ROLL WITH THE PUNCHES

If someone is telling you a joke and you
know the punch line, wait until they've
nearly finished, then tell them you've
heard it before.

THE CALMER SUTURE

Stitch people up as often as possible.
Especially your friends.

FORGET THE MOVIES—
ENJOY THE TALKIES

Go to a movie. Sit near other people.
Hold a conversation with a friend.

IN A WAY YOU'RE
SAVING THEM TIME

On the way out of the movie, if there's
a line waiting to go in, discuss the ending
in a loud voice with your friend.

SOUND ADVICE

Record the sound of a dentist's drill.
Play it at bedtime.

KNOW LIMITS

Recognize your limitations.
Then ignore them.

IT'S BETTER THAT
THEY SHOULD KNOW

Recognize other people's limitations.
Then tell people what they are.

DON'T YOU JUST HATE IT WHEN THAT HAPPENS?

Call your friends when they're out.
Hang up just after the answering
machine starts recording.

Repeat.

RUSH HOUR

Always travel during rush hour.
Pay your toll fee with a credit card.

A SALE
I

Go to a sale on the first day when
the crowds are the biggest.
Then buy something you'll
never, ever wear.

A SALE
2

Go to a sale near the end
when it's quieter.
Beat yourself up over all the bargains
you've missed.

SCANNER MANNERS

In the supermarket deface all the bar codes
of your items so they won't scan.

IF I DON'T DO IT...

Don't delegate. They'll only do it wrong.

ENCOURAGE COFFEE BREAKDOWNS

Switch the decaffeinated and caffeinated coffees around whenever you can.

DRIVE THEM MAD

Switch lanes often in your car.
Never use your turn signal.

CAN DO

Hide the can opener.
When you visit your friends' homes,
hide theirs.

COMPLICATE

The more things you must do
in life, the more things you own,
manage, or are responsible for,
the more things can go wrong.

THE BEST POLICY

Be honest.
All the time.
With everyone.
About everything.

THE BETTER POLICY

Lie.
All the time.
To everyone.
About everything.

BE RUDE

Practice rudeness,
not just to make others feel bad, but also
to make you feel bad about yourself.

It's a win-win situation.

NEVER FORGIVE

Forgiving is a sign of weakness.
People will despise you for it.

NURTURING IS GOOD

Nurture your grievances.
If you don't they'll die
and then whoever's done you wrong
will have got away with it.

EVEN IN THE
SMALLEST SPACES

Fart in confined spaces.
But only if other people are present.

CARPE DIEM

From the Latin "carpe"—to carp or whine,
and "diem"—meaning daily,
hence "carpe diem"—whine daily.

CAR PARK DIEM

When out driving, if you see
an opportunity to box someone in
by parking too close to them,
seize it.

REJECTION

Apply for jobs you're totally unsuited for.
Keep all the rejection letters to read
whenever you start to feel good about
yourself.

DIET HARD

Eat less fresh food.
Eat more things containing preservatives.
Preservatives are called preservatives
because they help you live longer.

LOST LOVE

Make a list of all the people
who've ever dumped you.
Contact them once a year and try
to restart the relationship.

GET LOST, LOVE

Make a list of all the people
you've ever dumped.
Contact them once a year and try
to restart the relationship.

THERE IS USE CRYING

Always buy milk in cartons you find
difficult to open.

BECOME A JUNKIE

Get a job writing junk mail.

AFTER HOURS

Always work late.
It'll make you feel tired, irritable,
and exploited.

WORKING LATE—THE DOUBLE WHAMMY

Always work late.
Everyone else in the company
will hate you for it.
Except your boss who will despise
your gullibility.

REJOICE IN SMALL PRINT

Small print annoys everyone.
The people who read it.
The people who don't read it.
Even the people who write it.

It's great stuff.

A FROWN WILL
NEVER LET YOU DOWN

A frown communicates both
disapproval of others and unhappiness
within yourself.

IS YOUR BAR
TOO LOW?

Often it's very hard to live up
to the standards we set for ourselves.
However, sometimes we do.
To ensure this never happens, make a habit
of constantly raising the standards
you set for yourself.

TAKE CREDIT

Take credit for successes that have
nothing to do with you.

YOU NEED THE RIGHT BACKING

If you spend most of your day sitting at
a desk, invest in a really cheap chair.
Make sure it doesn't give your
back any support.

TEMPERS FUGIT

Buy and wear a second watch.
Set it to beep every half hour so you can
panic about being behind schedule.

SCHEDULES

Make them whenever possible.
Include an unrealistic number of tasks.
Agonize over why you're constantly
falling behind.

HFZ

Make yourself a Humor Free Zone.
If you ever find yourself laughing at a
predicament you're in, go to the bathroom
and pull yourself together.

PERSPECTIVE AND PROPORTION

It is no coincidence that painting
got much better when artists discovered
perspective and proportion.

So avoid both.
They are no help at all to the
dedicated disciples of stress.

THE PRESENT TENSE

Really tense up all your muscles.
Try to stay this way all day.
If this proves impossible, you have yet
again failed at a really simple task.

IT DOES YOU CREDIT

Apply for as many credit cards as you can.
Max them out.
Then get more credit cards
and do the same.

IMPULSE DRIVE

Never resist an impulse purchase.
Research has shown that impulse purchases
are the ones most likely to cause regret the
minute you get home. They're also the
ones most likely to encourage marital
disharmony.

CULTIVATE PST

Postshopping Stress can easily
be cultivated.
For instance, after you've bought an
expensive item, call all the stores
to discover that you could have bought it
considerably cheaper elsewhere.

MORE HASTE

Just as you can be influenced by the group
around you, with a little determination
you can influence them. A simple
technique is to rush and nag everyone
into doing things faster than they want.

COMMUNICATION
BREAKDOWNS

If you are stressed, make sure
you communicate this to those around you.
Soon they'll be stressed too.

THE MEANING OF LIFE

Be mean. No one likes a meany.
Dedicated meanyness can really irritate
and annoy those around you. This
technique is especially recommended
to those who have, or are paid,
a lot of money.

TURN ON, TURN UP

Turn on and turn up all the
appliances in any room you are in.
Never turn anything off.

TURNIP

One day a week eat only turnips.

ALL THE FUN OF
THE UNFAIR

As a child whenever I used to wail,
"That's not fair,"
my mother used to reply,
"Life's not fair."

Why change things now?

THE FRESH FRUIT
STRATAGEM

Buy fresh fruit and put it in a bowl.
Then watch it rot.
This will make you feel bad because:
1. You're wasting money.
2. You're failing at something
that's good for you.

CREATE A
DEPRESSION BANK

Stockpile memories of things that
really depress you.
Remember them, relive them,
reflect on them.
Fit them into your daily routine.

OLD FLAMES CAN STILL BURN

Keep a photo of a past lover
somewhere your current love is
bound to find it.

HOW TO WIN AT LOSING
I

Buy small, expensive things
that are easy to lose.

HOW TO WIN AT LOSING
2

Buy large, expensive things
and find ways of losing them.

EDEN WAS
A GARDEN

Gardening is relaxing.
Never garden.

DON'T STOP

If you're not getting anywhere with
a task that is becoming increasingly
frustrating, don't stop.
On no account walk away from it.
Research shows that the more stressed
you are the more likely you are to solve
the problem.

THE TRUTH ABOUT
BUSINESS

In any business encounter, always
remember that the other person is out to
screw you.

THE TRUTH ABOUT BOSSES

At work, never forget that any initiative that comes from management is really a well-disguised way of getting you to work more for less money.

SMUG AS A BUG
IN A RUG

Be smug. Smug people are really annoying.
No one likes smug people.
In fact anthropologists have discovered
that in all societies, all over the world,
smug people are hated.

LEAVE LATE

When going anywhere make sure
you set off late.

Especially if you're going to an
important appointment.

NO ONE LIKES
A CRY BABY

Never cry. Crying is a sign of weakness.
In fact, only sissies cry.
It is far better to bottle up your
unhappiness inside you where it can grow
like a giant fungus deep within a rotting
tree stump.

EXPERIENCE
THE SUNRISE

Sunrise is a deeply spiritual and uplifting
time. However, if you stay up all night
to see it you'll be so tired you'll
see it for the disappointing everyday
event it really is.

Slash and Burn

Plants are soothing.
They make you feel closer to nature.
Never have them in the house.

Try not to have them in the garden.

EVERY CLOUD DOESN'T HAVE A SILVER LINING

Don't fall for this drivel. It's just deeply unscientific propaganda put out by optimists. In fact, it's more likely that every cloud has a lead lining which means all our reservoirs are full of poisoned water.

BE TOUCHY,
NOT TOUCHY-FEELY

Isolate yourself from human contact.
Shout at anyone who tries to invade your
personal space.

A TOUCHY EXCEPTION

The only time it is permissible to touch
someone is when that person has made it
clear they are uncomfortable with
physical contact.

PEANUTS ENVY

When entertaining guests make sure
to serve them a bowl of peanuts
as munchies, while keeping a bowl of
macadamia nuts for yourself.

BREATHE FASTER

The faster you breathe, the more air
you get. It's a way of getting one up on
those around you. You're breathing air that
should rightfully be theirs.

And they can't do anything about it.

DEPRESS YOURSELF EARLY

As soon as you wake up in the morning
turn on a radio news show.
News is always bad.
What better way to put you in the
right frame of mind for the day?

THE TIMES THEY
AREN'T A-CHANGING

You know the saying
"a change is as good as a rest"?
Well, it's a lie. Change invariably
makes things worse.

Resist it.

BECOME A POLITICIAN

DON'T ONLY WORRY
ABOUT BIG THINGS

Small things need to be worried about too.
And if you have no big things to worry
about, worry about two small things.
(The stress generated will be the same.)

GO SIP FROM THE
POISONED FOUNTAIN

Listen to gossip.
Pass it on to everybody.
And embellish it in the telling.

MAKE WAR, NOT LOVE

Try to replace lovemaking with arguing.
And if you find your arguments getting a
little routine, try spicing things up by
arguing in unusual locations.

HOME IS WHERE THE HEARTACHE IS

Move home. Twice a year.

Every year.

MARRIAGE GUIDANCE

Get married as often as possible.

HOW TO TURN WEDDING BELLS INTO A RIGHT DING-DONG

When getting married insist on having more guests on your side than your partner.

SWEET DREAMS

A double espresso just before bed
is always a winner.

CLEAR AIR TURBULENCE

Never "clear the air."
Instead investigate all the subtle nuances
of the word "fester."

THEY'RE JUST NOT
TRYING

When traveling abroad remember
foreigners can understand English if you
talk loudly and slowly.

"BUT I LOVE HIM/HER"

Constantly choose the wrong partner.
Always turn to the same friend for support
when things go wrong.

CONTEMPLATE
YOUR NOVEL

When reflecting on the many failures in
your life, remember how you've done
nothing about that novel you've always
said you were going to write.

PETS

Research shows that people with pets
live longer.
Never get a pet. And encourage your
friends' and neighbors' pets to run away.

THE LAST WORD

Always make sure you have the last word.

Raise the stakes by making that last word
"dickhead."

BORROWED
DISINTEREST

Never return things you borrow.

KEEP UP

Keep up with the Joneses.
Learn the names of everyone on your street.
Keep up with them too.

NO SMOKE WITHOUT IRE

1. Smoke.

2. Smoke cigars.

3. Smoke cigars in "No Smoking" areas.

USEFUL PHRASE

"Why did you do that?"

SHOPPING

Do your weekly shopping in a big
supermarket on a Saturday morning.
Take your children with you.
If you don't have any children
of your own, borrow some.

WHAT FRIENDS ARE FOR

Always borrow money from friends.
Forget or put off repaying it for as long
as possible.

SINGLED OUT

Ask single women if they've got
a boyfriend yet.

Repeat on Valentine's Day.

IT'S GOOD TO TALK

At dinner parties try to bring the
conversation around to sex, religion,
or politics.
Preferably all three.

COUNT YOUR BLESSINGS

Why?
You haven't got any.

Count your problems instead.

ROUTINES

Routines are good.
Have routines and stick to them religiously.
Refuse to change them for any reason,
no matter how reasonable.

BECAUSE THEY CAN'T CLOSE THEIR EARS

Cultivate an annoying voice.

CREATE A MEMOTOCRACY

If you work in an office, get into the habit
of communicating exclusively by memo.

NO ONE LIKES SLEEPING
IN A DAMP BED

Be a wet blanket.

CAPTAIN HOOK,
I PRESUME?

Never let yourself, or anyone else,
off the hook.

KNOW YOUR PLACE
I

Always remember that, in truth, you are
only a small, unimportant cog in a
massive machine you can't control.

KNOW YOUR PLACE
2

Always remember that you are, in truth,
the center of the universe,
the very sun that everything and everyone
else should revolve around.

IS ANYONE IN CHARGE?

Deal with bureaucracies as
often as you can.
Bureaucracies are the foundation
of stress creation.

THINK ABOUT IT

Why meditate when you can worry?
Worrying is meditation carried out
by realists.

LAUGHTER—THE WORST MEDICINE

The only time it is permissible to laugh is when you encounter the misfortune of others.

But you can only laugh in their presence.

BECOME A JUNK HUNK

Junk food will help you lead a rubbish life.
Eat it as often as you can.

BEDTIME READING

Write down your worries.
Read the list before you go to bed.

THE EARLY BIRD

Take offense early.
It saves time.

ADVICE ADDS SPICE

Take every opportunity to give others advice.
Especially on subjects of which you have
very little or no knowledge.

THE TRUTH

Recognize that true happiness depends
solely on how many material possessions
you own.

Act accordingly.

ADD ADDITIVES

Try to maximize your additive
consumption during the day.

RAISE YOUR VOICE

Shout at people at least twice a day.

SAVED

When working on a computer,
never save your work as you go.
This way, when you accidentally erase
something the whole day's effort will have
been wasted.

THE THEORY
OF RELATIVITY

If Einstein was correct
and everything is relative,
then it's all your parents' fault.
Blame them as often as you can.

THE EARNESTNESS
OF BEING IMPORTANT

Let both inferiors and superiors
know that you are important.
And that you're serious about it.

THE THREE P'S

Patronize.
Patronize.
Patronize.

THE INCOMPLETE CIRCLE

In a bar never buy a round.

UPGRADE YOUR
STEREO SYSTEM

Develop a system that reduces everyone
you encounter to a specific, crass
stereotype. Use this as a basis for all
conversations with them.

THE BEATEN TRACK

Never stray from the beaten track.
Because the beaten track is a track for the
beaten. And, face it, that's you.

A SUGGESTED
CAREER PATH

Get a job at a bank.
Rise to a high position.
Then implement a policy that
closes most of the money drawers
at the busiest times.

SEE THE LIGHT

Replace your bulbs with overhead,
neon-strip lights.

If you can get ones that flicker,
all the better.

Unreflexology

Buy shoes one size too small.

THE END OF FRIENDSHIP

Come to terms with the undeniable truth
that a friend is only an enemy you haven't
upset yet.

THE CHILD WITHIN

Get in touch with the child within you.
Not the one who sees the world with eyes
filled with wonder, but the one who sulks,
whines, and constantly demands attention.

Introduce this child to those around you.

THE BEST STRESSED
PEOPLE

Always criticize everyone's clothes.

SPARE TIME, OR
GOING SPARE TIME?

Take up hobbies you're no good at.

TIME ISN'T MONEY

When using an ATM
try out every transaction possible.
But only if there are people behind you.

NOTHING ANNOYS
LIKE NOTHING

Produce a book where one page is left
blank for no apparent reason other
than to perplex and short-change readers.

DIY

Research shows that by far the best time
for drilling holes in walls is early on a
Sunday morning.

IF AT FIRST YOU DON'T SUCCEED . . .

It must be someone else's fault.
Find them; blame them; make them pay.

THE GOLDEN RULE

Remember that there is absolutely no point
in talking about someone behind their back
unless they get to hear about it.

THE ORDER OF
THE BATH

Never clean it.

MOBILE PHONES

Enough said.

PSSST! DO YOU WANT
TO KNOW A SECRET?

Listen. Don't ask me how I found out,
but your colleagues who do the same
job as you are all getting paid a lot
more than you.

GRATE EXPECTATIONS

Constantly raise the hopes of those around
you that you're going to mend your ways.
Then take every opportunity to dash
those hopes.

FUTURE TENSE

You know the saying, "Don't worry,
it may never happen"?
Well, it's a lie. It will happen.
And knowing your luck, it will happen
more than once.

IT'S BETTER TO GIVE,
THEN RECEIVE

Buy extra copies of this book.
Give them to your friends as presents.
Then, when they express their thanks,
charge them full price
plus a handling fee.

ABOUT THE AUTHOR

Rohan Candappa's mother was born in Burma and
his father in Sri Lanka. He was born in Norbury,
South London, in 1962, so he can remember John
Noakes on *Blue Peter*, but not Christopher Trace.
His years of experience as an advertising copywriter
helped him become an authority on stress.
He is currently writing screenplays and lives in
North London with his actor wife, plus a blind cat
called Bump.